A Catholic Prayer Journal

This book is dedicated to our sweet Nicky.
We love you very much.

A Catholic Prayer Journal

By Jennifer & Travis Rainey

"Have no anxiety about anything, but in everything by prayer and supplication with thanksgiving let your requests be made known to God. And the peace of God, which passes all understanding, will keep your hearts and your minds in Christ Jesus."
Philippians 4:6-7

Dear Friends,

It is easy to become overwhelmed with all of the tasks of daily life. But, as St. Francis de Sales said, "Every one of us needs a half an hour of prayer each day, except when we are busy – then we need an hour." This book should help us with that goal.

Prayer is simply a conversation with God, and He is patiently waiting for us to talk to Him. Therefore, we should speak to Him on a regular basis, with all of our requests, to tell him what we are thankful for, to praise Him, and to ask for forgiveness.

In this book, each prayer page has space to write your prayers, as well as a quote from Holy Scripture or a saint. The back of the book has many Catholic prayers, including the Most Holy Rosary and the Divine Mercy Chaplet. There are also extra pages where you can list regular prayer requests and thanksgiving lists.

It is my prayer that this book will help to guide all of us into a richer daily prayer life.

Jennifer & Travis Rainey
May 2017

Immaculate Heart by C.B. Chambers

Date

_____

✝ _____

_____

_____

_____

_____

_____

_____

_____

_____

_____

I am thankful for

_____

_____

_____

I am praying for

_____

_____

_____

"Cheerfulness prepares a glorious mind for all the noblest acts."
St. Elizabeth Ann Seton

Date

I am thankful for

I am praying for

"Don't imagine that, if you had a great deal of time, you would spend more of it in prayer. Get rid of that idea; it is no hindrance to prayer to spend your time well." - St. Teresa of Avila

Date

_____

_____

_____

_____

_____

_____

_____

_____

_____

_____

_____

I am thankful for

_____

_____

_____

I am praying for

_____

_____

_____

"For God so loved the world that he gave his only Son, that whoever believes in him should not perish but have eternal life." John 3:16

Date _____

_____

_____

_____

_____

_____

_____

_____

_____

_____

_____

I am thankful for

- _____
- _____
- _____

I am praying for

- _____
- _____
- _____

"Love is shown more in deeds than in words."
St. Ignatius of Loyola

Date _____

_____

_____

_____

_____

_____

_____

_____

_____

_____

_____

I am thankful for

_____ _____

_____ _____

_____ _____

I am praying for

_____ _____

_____ _____

_____ _____

"Prayer is the place of refuge for every worry, a foundation for cheerfulness, a source of constant happiness, a protection against sadness."- St. John Chrysostom

Date

I am thankful for

I am praying for

"We know that in everything God works for good with those who love him, who are called according to his purpose."
Romans 8:28

Date

_____

_____

_____

_____

_____

_____

_____

_____

_____

I am thankful for

_____

_____

_____

I am praying for

_____

_____

_____

"Patience is the companion of wisdom."
St. Augustine of Hippo

Date

I am thankful for

I am praying for

"How often I failed in my duty to God because I was not leaning on the strong pillar of prayer."

St. Teresa of Avila

Date _____

_____

_____

_____

_____

_____

_____

_____

_____

_____

I am thankful for

_____

_____

_____

I am praying for

_____

_____

_____

"If God is for us, who is against us?"
Romans 8:31

Date

I am thankful for

I am praying for

"Don't get upset with your imperfections.... Simply surrender to the Power of God's Love, which is always greater than our weakness."- St. Francis De Sales

Date

_____

_____

_____

_____

_____

_____

_____

_____

_____

_____

I am thankful for

_____

_____

_____

I am praying for

_____

_____

_____

"Let us not waste time reflecting so much upon our troubles, either past or present... for they have less power to harm us when we disregard and ignore them." – St. Margaret Mary Alacoque

Date

I am thankful for

I am praying for

"Begin now... believe me, don't wait until tomorrow to begin becoming a saint." – St. Thérèse of Lisieux

Date _____

_____

_____

_____

_____

_____

_____

_____

_____

_____

I am thankful for

_____

_____

_____

I am praying for

_____

_____

_____

*"Act as if every day were the last of your life, and each action the
last you perform."*
St. Alphonsus Maria de Liguori

Date

I am thankful for

I am praying for

"God loves each of us as if there were only one of us."

Saint Augustine of Hippo

Date

_____

_____
_____
_____
_____
_____
_____
_____
_____

I am thankful for

I am praying for

_____   _____

_____   _____

_____   _____

"The longer the trial to which God subjects you, the greater the goodness in comforting you during the time of the trial and in the exaltation after the combat." – St. Padre Pio

Date

_____

_____

_____

_____

_____

_____

_____

_____

_____

_____

_____

_____

I am thankful for

_____

_____

_____

I am praying for

_____

_____

_____

"Do not be anxious about your life, what you shall eat or what you shall drink, nor about your body, what you shall put on. Is not life more than food, and the body more than clothing?"
Matthew 6:25

Date _____

_____

_____

_____

_____

_____

_____

_____

_____

_____

I am thankful for

_____

_____

_____

I am praying for

_____

_____

_____

"While the world changes, the cross stands firm."
St. Bruno

Date

I am thankful for

I am praying for

"To maintain a joyful family requires much from both the parents and the children. Each member of the family has to become, in a special way, the servant of the others." - St. John Paul II

Date

_____

_____

_____

_____

_____

_____

_____

_____

_____

_____

_____

_____

I am thankful for

_____

_____

_____

I am praying for

_____

_____

_____

"Keep your heart in peace and let nothing trouble you, not even your faults... for God's dwelling is in peace."

St. Margaret Mary Alacoque

Date

I am thankful for

I am praying for

"Our Lord has created persons for all states in life, and in all of them we see people who achieved sanctity by fulfilling their obligations well." – St. Anthony Mary Claret

Date

_____

_____

_____

_____

_____

_____

_____

_____

_____

_____

I am thankful for

_____

_____

_____

I am praying for

_____

_____

_____

"The first end I propose in our daily work is to do the will of God;
secondly, to do it in the manner He wills it; and thirdly to do it
because it is His will." – St. Elizabeth Ann Seton

Date _____

_____

_____

_____

_____

_____

_____

_____

_____

_____

_____

I am thankful for

- _____
- _____
- _____

I am praying for

- _____
- _____
- _____

"Joy, with peace, is the sister of charity. Serve the Lord with laughter." – St. Padre Pio

Date _____

✝ _____

_____

_____

_____

_____

_____

_____

_____

_____

I am thankful for

- _____
- _____
- _____

I am praying for

- _____
- _____
- _____

"By the anxieties and worries of this life Satan tries to dull man's heart and make a dwelling for himself there." - St. Francis of Assisi

Date _____

_____

_____

_____

_____

_____

_____

_____

_____

_____

_____

I am thankful for

_____

_____

_____

I am praying for

_____

_____

_____

"Maintain a spirit of peace and you will save a thousand souls."
St. Seraphim of Sarov

Date

I am thankful for

I am praying for

"Love ought to consist of deeds more than of words."

St. Ignatius of Loyola

Date

_____

_____

_____

_____

_____

_____

_____

_____

_____

_____

_____

I am thankful for

_____

_____

_____

I am praying for

_____

_____

_____

"Do not worry over things that generate preoccupation and anxiety. One thing only is necessary: To lift up your spirit and love to God." - St. Padre Pio

Date

_____

_____

_____

_____

_____

_____

_____

_____

_____

_____

I am thankful for

- _____
- _____
- _____

I am praying for

- _____
- _____
- _____

"If you are what you should be, you will set the whole world ablaze!" – Saint Catherine of Siena

Date

_____

_____

_____

_____

_____

_____

_____

_____

_____

_____

I am thankful for

_____

_____

_____

I am praying for

_____

_____

_____

"Jesus, help me to simplify my life by learning what you want me to be and becoming that person."
Saint Thérèse of Lisieux

Date

I am thankful for

I am praying for

"If you believe what you like in the gospels, and reject what you don't like, it is not the gospel you believe, but yourself."

Saint Augustine of Hippo

Date

_____

_____

_____

_____

_____

_____

_____

_____

_____

_____

_____

_____

I am thankful for

_____

_____

_____

I am praying for

_____

_____

_____

"Have no anxiety about anything, but in everything by prayer and supplication with thanksgiving let your requests be made known to God." - Philippians 4:6

Date

_____

_____

_____

_____

_____

_____

_____

_____

_____

_____

I am thankful for   I am praying for

_____   _____

_____   _____

_____   _____

"Let nothing disturb you, nothing frighten you; all things are passing; God never changes."
St. Teresa of Avila

Date _____

_____

_____

_____

_____

_____

_____

_____

_____

_____

_____

_____

_____

I am thankful for

- _____
- _____
- _____

I am praying for

- _____
- _____
- _____

"To put into practice the teachings of our holy faith, it is not enough to convince ourselves that they are true; we must love them. Love united to faith makes us practice our religion."
St. Alphonsus Liguori

Date _____

_____

_____

_____

_____

_____

_____

_____

_____

_____

I am thankful for   I am praying for

_____   _____

_____   _____

_____   _____

"Joy is a net of love by which we catch souls."
St. Teresa of Calcutta

Date

I am thankful for

I am praying for

"Truth always ends by victory; it is not unassailable, but invincible." – *St. Ignatius of Loyola*

Date _____

_____

_____

_____

_____

_____

_____

_____

_____

_____

_____

_____

I am thankful for

_____

_____

_____

I am praying for

_____

_____

_____

"For pity's sake, don't start meeting troubles halfway."

St. Teresa of Avila

Date _____

_____

_____

_____

_____

_____

_____

_____

_____

_____

_____

_____

I am thankful for

I am praying for

_____

_____

_____

_____

_____

_____

"We know that (God) gives us every grace, every abundant grace; and though we are so weak of ourselves, this grace is able to carry us through every obstacle and difficulty."
St. Elizabeth Ann Seton

Date

_____

✝

_____

_____

_____

_____

_____

_____

_____

_____

I am thankful for

_____

_____

_____

I am praying for

_____

_____

_____

"I wish not merely to be called Christian, but also to be Christian."
St. Ignatius of Antioch

Date _____

_____

_____

_____

_____

_____

_____

_____

_____

_____

_____

I am thankful for

- _____
- _____
- _____

I am praying for

- _____
- _____
- _____

"All the wealth in the world cannot be compared with the happiness of living together happily united."

Blessed Margaret d'Youville

Date

I am thankful for

I am praying for

"The riddles of God are more satisfying than the solutions of man." – G.K. Chesterton

Date

I am thankful for

I am praying for

"Humility is the foundation of all the other virtues hence, in the soul in which this virtue does not exist there cannot be any other virtue except in mere appearance." – Saint Augustine of Hippo

Date

_____

_____

_____

_____

_____

_____

_____

_____

_____

_____

I am thankful for

I am praying for

_____

_____

_____

_____

_____

_____

"The world's thy ship and not thy home."
St. Thérèse of Lisieux

Date

I am thankful for

I am praying for

"It is better to be a child of God than king of the whole world."

St. Aloysius Gonzaga

Date

_____

I am thankful for

I am praying for

"The secret of happiness is to live moment by moment and to thank God for all that He, in His goodness, sends to us day after day."
St. Gianna Molla

Date

I am thankful for

I am praying for

"Sweetest Lord, make me appreciative of the dignity of my high vocation, and its many responsibilities. Never permit me to disgrace it by giving way to coldness, unkindness, or impatience."
St. Teresa of Calcutta

Date _____

_____

_____

_____

_____

_____

_____

_____

_____

_____

I am thankful for

- _____
- _____
- _____

I am praying for

- _____
- _____
- _____

"My past, O Lord, to Your mercy; my present, to Your love; my future to Your providence."
St. Padre Pio

Date

_____

_____

_____

_____

_____

_____

_____

_____

_____

_____

_____

_____

_____

I am thankful for

_____

_____

_____

I am praying for

_____

_____

_____

"Nothing is more beautiful than love. Indeed, faith and hope will
end when we die, whereas love, that is, charity,
will last for eternity."
Bl. Pier Giorgio Frassati

Date

_____

_____

_____

_____

_____

_____

_____

_____

_____

_____

I am thankful for

_____

_____

_____

I am praying for

_____

_____

_____

"Pray, hope, and don't worry. Worry is useless. God is merciful and will hear your prayer."
St. Padre Pio

Date

I am thankful for

I am praying for

"Jacob did not cease to be a Saint because he had to attend to his flocks." – St. Teresa of Avila

Date

I am thankful for

I am praying for

"Whenever anything disagreeable or displeasing happens to you, remember Christ crucified and be silent."
St. John of the Cross

Date

_____

_____

_____

_____

_____

_____

_____

_____

_____

_____

I am thankful for

_____

_____

_____

I am praying for

_____

_____

_____

"Love begins by taking care of the closest ones – the ones at home."
St. Teresa of Calcutta

Date _____

_____

_____

_____

_____

_____

_____

_____

_____

_____

_____

_____

I am thankful for   I am praying for

_____   _____

_____   _____

_____   _____

"I can do all things in him who strengthens me."
Philippians 4:13

Date

_____

_____

_____

_____

_____

_____

_____

_____

_____

_____

_____

I am thankful for

I am praying for

_____

_____

_____

_____

_____

_____

_____

_____

_____

*"Miracles are not contrary to nature, but only contrary to
what we know about nature."*
Saint Augustine of Hippo

Date ⁜

I am thankful for

I am praying for

"If you wish to be pleasing to God and happy here below, be in all things united to His will." – St. Alphonsus Liguori

Date _____

_____

_____

_____

_____

_____

_____

_____

_____

_____

_____

I am thankful for   I am praying for

_____   _____

_____   _____

_____   _____

*"In comparison with the love of Jesus, everything else is secondary.
And without the love of Jesus, everything else is useless."*

St. John Paul II

Date

I am thankful for

I am praying for

"You pay God a compliment by asking great things of Him."
St. Teresa of Avila

Date

I am thankful for

I am praying for

"Therefore do not be anxious about tomorrow, for tomorrow will be anxious for itself. Let the day's own trouble be sufficient for the day." – Matthew 6:34

Date

I am thankful for

I am praying for

"Take for your motto: Love has conquered me, it alone shall possess my heart."
St. Margaret Mary Alacoque

Date

_____

_____

_____

_____

_____

_____

_____

_____

_____

_____

_____

I am thankful for

I am praying for

"The gate of heaven is very low; only the humble can enter it."
St. Elizabeth Ann Seton

Date

_____

✝

_____

_____

_____

_____

_____

_____

_____

_____

_____

I am thankful for

- _____
- _____
- _____

I am praying for

- _____
- _____
- _____

"When you look at the crucifix, you understand how much Jesus loved you then. When you look at the Sacred Host, you understand how much Jesus loves you now." – St. Teresa of Calcutta

Date _____

_____

_____
_____
_____
_____
_____
_____
_____
_____

I am thankful for	I am praying for
_____	_____
_____	_____
_____	_____

"We must pray without tiring, for the salvation of mankind does not depend upon material success... but on Jesus alone."
St. Frances Xavier Cabrini

Date _____

_____

_____
_____
_____
_____
_____
_____
_____
_____
_____

I am thankful for   I am praying for

_____   _____
_____   _____
_____   _____

"Spread love everywhere you go: first of all in your own house.
Give love to your children, to your wife or husband,
to a next-door neighbor."
St. Teresa of Calcutta

Date

I am thankful for

I am praying for

"The best way to acquire true dignity is to wash one's own clothes
and boil one's own pot."
St. Francis Xavier

Date _____

_____

_____

_____

_____

_____

_____

_____

_____

_____

_____

I am thankful for

_____

_____

_____

I am praying for

_____

_____

_____

"Like Our Lady, remain at the Cross of Jesus, and you will never be deprived of comfort."
St. Padre Pio

Date _____

_____

_____

_____

_____

_____

_____

_____

_____

_____

_____

_____

I am thankful for

_____

_____

_____

I am praying for

_____

_____

_____

"They who wait for the LORD shall renew their strength, they shall mount up with wings like eagles, they shall run and not be weary, they shall walk and not faint." – Isaiah 40:31

Date

_____

_____

_____

_____

_____

_____

_____

_____

_____

_____

I am thankful for   I am praying for

_____   _____

_____   _____

_____   _____

"For me prayer is a surge of the heart, it is a simple look towards Heaven, it is a cry of recognition and of love, embracing both trial and joy."
St. Therese of Lisieux

Date

_____

_____

_____

_____

_____

_____

_____

_____

_____

_____

_____

_____

I am thankful for

- _____
- _____
- _____

I am praying for

- _____
- _____
- _____

"If certain thoughts bother you, it is devil who causes you to worry, and not God, Who, being the spirit of peace, grants you tranquility."
St. Padre Pio

Date

I am thankful for

I am praying for

"God is a spring of living water which flows unceasingly into the hearts of those who pray."
St. Louis de Montfort

Date _____

_____

_____

_____

_____

_____

_____

_____

_____

_____

_____

I am thankful for

I am praying for

*"Can You see that as soon as the day breaks I think of You?
As evening comes, I am near You.
I am near You at every moment. I love You, Jesus!"*
St. Gemma Galgani

Date

I am thankful for

I am praying for

"Learn the heart of God from the word of God."
Pope St. Gregory

Date

_____

_____

_____

_____

_____

_____

_____

_____

_____

_____

_____

I am thankful for

_____

_____

_____

I am praying for

_____

_____

_____

"What does the poor man do at the rich man's door, the sick man in the presence of his physician, the thirsty man at a limpid stream? What they do, I do before the Eucharistic God. I pray. I adore. I love." – St. Francis of Assisi

Date

_____

_____

_____

_____

_____

_____

_____

_____

_____

_____

_____

I am thankful for

_____

_____

_____

I am praying for

_____

_____

_____

"Mount Calvary is the academy of love."
St. Francis de Sales

Date

I am thankful for

I am praying for

"Let no one ever come to you without leaving better and happier. Be the living expression of God's kindness: kindness in your face, kindness in your eyes, kindness in your smile, kindness in your warm greeting." – St. Teresa of Calcutta

Date

_____

_____

_____

_____

_____

_____

_____

_____

_____

_____

I am thankful for

I am praying for

"You can win more converts with a spoonful of honey than with a barrelful of vinegar."
St. Francis de Sales

Date

I am thankful for

I am praying for

"One must see God in everyone."
St. Catherine Laboure

Date _____

_____

_____

_____

_____

_____

_____

_____

_____

_____

_____

I am thankful for

- _____
- _____
- _____

I am praying for

- _____
- _____
- _____

"He who desires nothing but God is rich and happy."
St. Alphonsus Liguori

Date _____

_____

_____

_____

_____

_____

_____

_____

_____

_____

_____

I am thankful for   I am praying for

_____   _____

_____   _____

_____   _____

*"Make frequent visits to Jesus in the Blessed Sacrament and the
devil will be powerless against you."*
St. John Bosco

Date

I am thankful for

I am praying for

"When one does one's own duty, one must not be concerned, because God's help will not be lacking."
St. Gianna Molla

Date _____

_____

_____
_____
_____
_____
_____
_____
_____
_____
_____

I am thankful for   I am praying for

_____   _____
_____   _____
_____   _____

"Leave sadness to those in the world. We who work for God should be lighthearted."
St. Leonard of Port Maurice

Date

_____

_____

_____

_____

_____

_____

_____

_____

_____

_____

_____

I am thankful for

_____

_____

_____

I am praying for

_____

_____

_____

"Fear not because God is with you."
St. Padre Pio

Date

I am thankful for

I am praying for

"Also in suffering, let us say: Thanks be to God."
St. Gianna Molla

Date ....

....

....

....

....

....

....

....

....

....

....

I am thankful for

....

....

....

I am praying for

....

....

....

"We do not have to talk very much in order to pray well. We know that God is there in His holy tabernacle; let us open our hearts to Him; let us rejoice in His Presence: This is the best prayer."
St. John Vianney

Date

I am thankful for

I am praying for

"Let prayer delight thee more than disputations, and the charity
which buildeth up more than the
knowledge which puffeth up."
St. Robert Bellarmine

Date

_____

_____

_____

_____

_____

_____

_____

_____

_____

_____

I am thankful for

I am praying for

"When we pray, the voice of the heart must be heard more than
proceedings from the mouth."
St. Bonaventure

Date

_____

_____

_____

_____

_____

_____

_____

_____

_____

_____

_____

_____

I am thankful for

_____

_____

_____

I am praying for

_____

_____

_____

"He who labors as he prays lifts his heart to God with his hands."
St. Benedict of Nursia

Date

I am thankful for

I am praying for

"Suffering borne in the will quietly and patiently is a continual,
very powerful prayer before God."
St. Jane Frances de Chantal

Date

_____

_____

_____

_____

_____

_____

_____

_____

_____

_____

I am thankful for

_____

_____

_____

I am praying for

_____

_____

_____

"Mental prayer is nothing else but being on terms of friendship with God, frequently conversing in secret with Him."
St. Teresa of Avila

Date

I am thankful for

I am praying for

"The prayer of the sick person is his patience and his acceptance of his sickness for the love of Jesus Christ. Make sickness itself a prayer, for there is none more powerful, save martyrdom!"
St Francis de Sales

Date

_____

_____

_____

_____

_____

_____

_____

_____

_____

_____

I am thankful for

_____

_____

_____

I am praying for

_____

_____

_____

*"Our hearts were made for You, O Lord, and they are restless
until they rest in you."*
St. Augustine of Hippo

Date

_____

_____

_____

_____

_____

_____

_____

_____

_____

_____

_____

I am thankful for

_____

_____

_____

I am praying for

_____

_____

_____

"The nation doesn't simply need what we have.
It needs what we are."
St. Teresa Benedicta (Edith Stein)

Date

I am thankful for

I am praying for

"Every one of us needs a half an hour of prayer each day, except when we are busy – then we need an hour."
Saint Francis de Sales

Date

_____

_____

_____

_____

_____

_____

_____

_____

_____

_____

I am thankful for

_____

_____

_____

I am praying for

_____

_____

_____

"It is better to say one Our Father fervently and devoutly than a thousand with no devotion and full of distraction."
Saint Edmund

Date

I am thankful for

I am praying for

"Silence is God's first language."
Saint John of the Cross

Date

I am thankful for

I am praying for

"Apart from the cross, there is no other ladder by which we may get to heaven."
St. Rose of Lima

Date

I am thankful for

I am praying for

"There are more tears shed over answered prayers than over unanswered prayers."
St. Teresa of Avila

Date

I am thankful for

I am praying for

"How beautiful is the family that recites the Rosary every evening." – Saint John Paul II

Date

_____

_____

_____

_____

_____

_____

_____

_____

_____

_____

I am thankful for

_____

_____

_____

I am praying for

_____

_____

_____

*"From silly devotions and sour-faced saints,
good Lord, deliver us!"*
St. Teresa of Avila

Date

I am thankful for

I am praying for

"Until we have acquired genuine prayer, we are like people
teaching children to begin to walk."
St. Margaret Mary Alocoque

Date _____

_____

_____

_____

_____

_____

_____

_____

_____

I am thankful for

_____

_____

_____

I am praying for

_____

_____

_____

*"You cannot be half a saint; you must be a
whole saint or no saint at all."*
St. Therese of Lisieux

Date

I am thankful for

I am praying for

"We always find that those who walked closest to Christ were those who had to bear the greatest trials."
St. Teresa of Avila

Date _____

_____

_____

_____

_____

_____

_____

_____

_____

_____

I am thankful for

_____

_____

_____

I am praying for

_____

_____

_____

"When you approach the tabernacle remember that He has been waiting for you for twenty centuries."
St. Josemaria Escriva

Catholic Prayers

The Prayer by William-Adolphe Bouguereau

The Our Father

Our Father who art in Heaven, hallowed be Thy name; Thy Kingdom come; Thy will be done on earth as it is in Heaven. Give us this day our daily bread; and forgive us our trespasses as we forgive those who trespass against us; and lead us not into temptation, but deliver us from evil. Amen.

The Hail Mary

Hail Mary, full of grace! The Lord is with thee; blessed art thou among women, and blessed is the fruit of thy womb, Jesus. Holy Mary, Mother of God, pray for us sinners, now and at the hour of our death. Amen.

The Glory Be

Glory be to the Father, and to the Son, and to the Holy Spirit. As it was in the beginning, is now, and ever shall be, world without end. Amen.

The Fatima Prayer

O my Jesus, forgive us our sins, save us from the fires of hell, and lead all souls to Heaven, especially those most in need of Thy mercy. Amen.

Grace Before Meals

Bless us, O Lord, and these Thy gifts, which we are about to receive from Thy bounty, through Christ our Lord. Amen.

Grace After Meals

We give Thee thanks for all your benefits, O Almighty God, Who lives and reigns forever; and may the souls of the faithful departed, through the mercy of God, rest in peace. Amen.

Hail, Holy Queen

Hail, holy Queen, mother of mercy, our life, our sweetness, and our hope. To thee do we cry, poor banished children of Eve. To thee do we send up our sighs mourning and weeping in this valley of tears. Turn then, most gracious advocate, thine eyes of mercy toward us, and after this our exile show us the blessed fruit of thy womb, Jesus.
O clement, O loving, O sweet Virgin Mary.

Pray for us, O Holy Mother of God.

That we may be made worthy of the promises of Christ.

The Divine Praises

Blessed be God.
Blessed be his Holy Name.
Blessed be Jesus Christ, true God and true Man.
Blessed be the Name of Jesus.
Blessed be his most Sacred Heart.
Blessed be his most Precious Blood.
Blessed be Jesus in the most Holy Sacrament of the Altar.
Blessed be the Holy Spirit, the Paraclete.
Blessed be the great Mother of God, Mary most holy.
Blessed be her holy and Immaculate Conception.
Blessed be her glorious Assumption.
Blessed be the name of Mary, Virgin and Mother.
Blessed be St. Joseph, her most chaste spouse.
Blessed be God in his angels and in his saints.

The Morning Offering

O Jesus, through the Immaculate Heart of Mary, I offer You my prayers, works, joys and sufferings of this day for all the intentions of Your Sacred Heart, in union with the Holy Sacrifice of the Mass throughout the world, in reparation for my sins, for the intentions of all my relatives and friends, and in particular for the intentions of the Holy Father. Amen.

Memorare

Remember, O most gracious Virgin Mary, that never was it known that anyone who fled to thy protection, implored thy help, or sought thine intercession was left unaided.

Inspired by this confidence, I fly unto thee, O Virgin of virgins, my mother; to thee do I come, before thee I stand, sinful and sorrowful. O Mother of the Word Incarnate, despise not my petitions, but in thy mercy hear and answer me. Amen.

The Act of Contrition

O my God, I am heartily sorry for having offended Thee, and I detest all my sins, because I dread the loss of Heaven and the pains of Hell; but most of all because they offend Thee, my God, Who art all good and deserving of all my love. I firmly resolve, with the help of Thy grace, to confess my sins, to do penance and to amend my life. Amen.

Prayer to Saint Michael the Archangel

Saint Michael the Archangel, defend us in battle. Be our defense against the wickedness and snares of the Devil. May God rebuke him, we humbly pray, and do thou, O Prince of the Heavenly hosts, by the power of God, thrust into hell Satan, and all the evil spirits, who prowl about the world seeking the ruin of souls. Amen.

The Creed

I believe in God, the Father almighty, Creator of Heaven and earth, and in Jesus Christ, His only Son, our Lord. He was conceived by the Holy Spirit, and born of the Virgin Mary. He suffered under Pontius Pilate, was crucified, died and was buried. He descended into hell. On the third day He rose again. He ascended into Heaven, and is seated at the right hand of God the Father Almighty. He will come again to judge the living and the dead.

I believe in the Holy Spirit, the Holy Catholic Church, the communion of saints, the forgiveness of sins, the resurrection of the body, and life everlasting. Amen.

The Guardian Angel Prayer

Angel of God, my guardian dear, to whom God's love commits me here, ever this day be at my side to light and guard, to rule and guide. Amen.

The Holy Rosary

1. Make the Sign of the Cross and say, "In the name of the Father, and of the Son, and of the Holy Spirit. Amen."

2. Say the Creed.

3. Say one Our Father, three Hail Marys, and one Glory Be.

4. Announce the first Mystery (look on the next page for the Mysteries). Then pray one Our Father, ten Hail Marys, one Glory Be, and one Fatima Prayer while meditating on the Mystery.

5. Then pray one Our Father, ten Hail Marys, one Glory Be, and one Fatima Prayer for each Mystery.

6. After you have completed all the decades, say the Hail, Holy Queen.

7. Make the Sign of the Cross and say, "In the Name of the Father, and of the Son, and of the Holy Spirit. Amen."

The Mysteries of the Rosary

The Joyful Mysteries (Mondays and Saturdays, and Sundays during Advent and Christmas):

1. The Annunciation
2. The Visitation
3. The Nativity
4. The Presentation
5. The Finding of Jesus in the Temple

The Luminous Mysteries (Thursdays):

1. Baptism in the Jordan
2. The Wedding at Cana
3. Proclamation of the Kingdom
4. The Transfiguration
5. Institution of the Eucharist

The Sorrowful Mysteries (Tuesdays and Fridays, and Sundays during Lent):

1. Agony in the Garden
2. Scourging at the Pillar
3. Crowning with Thorns
4. Carrying of the Cross
5. The Crucifixion

The Glorious Mysteries (Wednesdays and Sundays):

1. The Resurrection
2. The Ascension
3. The Descent of the Holy Spirit
4. The Assumption of the Blessed Virgin Mary
5. The Coronation of the Blessed Virgin Mary

The 15 Promises of the Holy Rosary

The Blessed Mother gave Saint Dominic and Blessed Alan de la Roche promises that she assured them were given to those who recite the Holy Rosary faithfully.

Here are the promises:

1. Whosoever shall faithfully serve me by the recitation of the Rosary shall receive signal graces.

2. I promise my special protection and the greatest graces to all those who shall recite the Rosary.

3. The Rosary shall be a powerful armor against hell; it will destroy vice, decrease sin and defeat heresies.

4. It will cause good works to flourish; it will obtain for souls the abundant mercy of God; it will withdraw the hearts of men from the love of the world and its vanities, and will lift them to the desire for Eternal Things. Oh, that souls would sanctify themselves by this means.

5. The soul which recommends itself to me by the recitation of the Rosary shall not perish.

6. Whosoever shall recite the Rosary devoutly, applying himself to the consideration of its Sacred Mysteries shall never be conquered by misfortune. God will not chastise him in His justice; he shall not perish by an unprovided death; if he be just he shall remain in the grace of God, and become worthy of Eternal Life.

7. Whoever shall have a true devotion for the Rosary shall not die without the Sacraments of the Church.

8. Those who are faithful to recite the Rosary shall have during their life and at their death the Light of God and the plenitude of His Graces; at the moment of death they shall participate in the Merits of the Saints in Paradise.

9. I shall deliver from Purgatory those who have been devoted to the Rosary.

10. The faithful children of the Rosary shall merit a high degree of Glory in Heaven.

11. You shall obtain all you ask of me by recitation of the Rosary.

12. All those who propagate the Holy Rosary shall be aided by me in their necessities.

13. I have obtained from my Divine Son that all the advocates of the Rosary shall have for intercessors the entire Celestial Court during their life and at the hour of death.

14. All who recite the Rosary are my Sons, and brothers of my Only Son Jesus Christ.

15. Devotion to my Rosary is a great sign of predestination.

Quotes about the
Holy Rosary

"The Rosary is a powerful weapon to put the demons to flight and to keep oneself from sin…. If you desire peace in your hearts, in your homes and in your country, assemble each evening to recite the Rosary. Let not even one day pass without saying it, no matter how burdened you may be with many cares and labors."
– Pope Pius XI

"How beautiful is the family that recites the Rosary every evening." - Saint John Paul II

"Among all the devotions approved by the Church none has been so favored by so many miracles as the devotion of the Most Holy Rosary."
– Blessed Pius IX

"You always leave the Rosary for later, and you end up not saying it at all because you are sleepy. If there is no other time, say it in the street without letting anybody notice it. It will, moreover, help you to have presence of God."
– Saint Josemaria Escriva

"The Rosary is the 'weapon' for these times."
– Saint Padre Pio

"When people love and recite the Rosary, they find it makes them better."
– Saint Anthony Mary Claret

"Say the Rosary every day to obtain world peace."
– Our Lady of Fátima

"There is no problem, I tell you, no matter how difficult it is, that we cannot solve by the prayer of the Holy Rosary."
– Sister Lúcia de Jesus Rosa dos Santos (seer of Fátima)

"If you say the Rosary faithfully until death, I do assure you that, in spite of the gravity of your sins, you shall receive a never-fading crown of glory. Even if you are on the brink of damnation... sooner or later you will be converted and will amend your life and will save your soul, if – and mark well what I say – if you say the Holy Rosary devoutly every day until death for the purpose of knowing the truth and obtaining contrition and pardon for your sins."
– Saint Louis de Montfort

"[The Rosary] is one of the greatest secrets to have come down from Heaven."
– Saint Louis de Montfort

"The Rosary can bring families through all dangers and evils."
– Servant of God Patrick Peyton

The 12 Promises of
the Sacred Heart of Jesus

We can practice devotion to the Sacred Heart of Jesus by displaying His Sacred Heart prominently in our homes, having our houses Consecrated to the Sacred Heart and by making the Nine First Fridays in honor of Jesus' Sacred Heart. The following are the promises that Jesus gave to Saint Margaret Mary Alacoque for those who are devoted to His Sacred Heart:

1. I will give them all the graces necessary in their state of life.

2. I will give peace in their families and will unite families that are divided.

3. I will console them in all their troubles.

4. I will be their refuge during life and above all in death.

5. I will bestow the blessings of Heaven on all their enterprises.

6. Sinners shall find in my Heart the source and infinite ocean of mercy.

7. Tepid souls shall become fervent.

8. Fervent souls shall rise quickly to great perfection.

9. I will bless those places wherein the image of My Heart shall be exposed and honored and will imprint My love on the hearts of those who would wear this image on their person. I will also destroy in them all disordered movements.

10. I will give to priests who are animated by a tender devotion to my Divine Heart the gift of touching the most hardened hearts.

11. Those who promote this devotion shall have their names written in my Heart, never to be effaced.

12. I promise you in the excessive mercy of my Heart that my all-powerful love will grant to all those who communicate on the First Friday in nine consecutive months, the grace of final penitence: they will not die in my disgrace, nor without receiving their Sacraments. My Divine Heart shall be their safe refuge in this last moment.

The Divine Mercy Chaplet

Step 1 – Using a Rosary, begin at the cross by making the Sign of the Cross.

(Optional Opening Prayer)
You expired, Jesus, but the source of life gushed forth for souls, and the ocean of mercy opened up for the whole world. O Fount of Life, unfathomable Divine Mercy, envelop the whole world and empty Yourself out upon us.

Step 2 - O Blood and Water, which gushed forth from the Heart of Jesus as a fountain of Mercy for us, I trust in You! (Repeat three times)

Step 3 – On the three beads of the Rosary, pray the Our Father, the Hail Mary and the Apostles' Creed.

Step 4 – Begin each decade with the Our Father beads by praying this prayer:

Eternal Father, I offer You the Body and Blood, Soul and Divinity of Your dearly beloved Son, Our Lord Jesus Christ, in atonement for our sins and those of the whole world.

Step 5 – Complete the decade on the 10 Hail Mary beads by praying this prayer:

For the sake of His Sorrowful Passion, have mercy on us and on the whole world.

Repeat steps 4 and 5 for each decade.

Step 6 – After praying all five decades, pray the following prayer 3 times:

Holy God, Holy Mighty One, Holy Immortal One, have mercy on us and on the whole world.

Step 7 – (Optional Closing Prayer)
Eternal God, in whom mercy is endless and the treasury of compassion inexhaustible, look kindly upon us, and increase Your mercy in us, that in difficult moments, we might not despair nor become despondent, but with great confidence, submit ourselves to Your holy will, which is Love and Mercy itself.

Amen.

The Seven Sorrows Chaplet

According to St. Bridget of Sweden's (1303-1373) visions, the Blessed Virgin promised to grant seven graces to those who meditate daily on her Sorrows:

- "I will grant peace to their families."
- "They will be enlightened about the divine Mysteries."
- "I will console them in their pains and will accompany them in their work."
- "I will give them as much as they ask for as long as it does not oppose the adorable will of my divine Son or the sanctification of their souls."
- "I will defend them in their spiritual battles with the infernal enemy and I will protect them at every instant of their lives."
- "I will visibly help them at the moment of their death-- they will see the face of their mother."
- "I have obtained this grace from my divine Son, that those who propagate this devotion to my tears and dolors will be taken directly from this earthly life to eternal happiness, since all their sins will be forgiven and my Son will be their eternal consolation and joy."

How to Pray the Seven Sorrows (Dolors) Chaplet:

Step 1 – (Optional) Make an Act of Contrition

Step 2 – Pray one Our Father and seven Hail Marys for each of Mary's Sorrows.

> **The First Sorrow:** The Prophecy of Simeon (Luke 2:25-35)

> **The Second Sorrow:** The Flight Into Egypt (Matthew 2:13-15)

> **The Third Sorrow:** The Child Jesus Lost in the Temple (Luke 2:41-50)

> **The Fourth Sorrow** Mary Meeting Jesus as He Carries the Cross

> **The Fifth Sorrow** Mary at the Foot of the Cross (John 19:25-30)

> **The Sixth Sorrow** Mary receives the Body of Jesus

> **The Seventh Sorrow:** Jesus' Burial (Luke 23:50-56)

Step 3 – Pray three Hail Marys in honor of the Blessed Mother's Tears. Pray one Our Father, Hail Mary, and one Glory Be for the Holy Father's intentions. Finally, pray "Virgin Most Sorrowful, Pray for Us" three times.

My Favorite Bible Verses

My Favorite Bible Verses

Regular Prayer Intentions

Regular Prayer Intentions

_____

_____

_____

_____

_____

_____

_____

_____

_____

_____

I am thankful for...

_____

_____

_____

_____

_____

_____

_____

_____

_____

I am thankful for...

_____

_____

_____

_____

_____

_____

_____

_____

_____

_____

I am thankful for...

_____

_____

_____

_____

_____

_____

_____

_____

_____

I am thankful for...

Notes

Notes